proudly presents:

PuRe ChAoS

Cover art by Ashley Keenan

WARNING:

The contents in this book may be difficult for some to handle. There is profanity, talk of depression, alcoholism, suicide, amongst others. It is recommended that readers be 18+. This book in no way promotes self-harm. If you are struggling, please know that you are NOT alone and there is help. You can text or call 988, call 1-800-273-TALK (8255, veterans press 1), text TALK to 741741, or go online and chat at www.988lifeline.org and select the live chat option. You have every reason to stay alive, you are never alone! ♥

Acknowledgements

I would like to take a moment to thank my mother, Katrina, who has always been my biggest cheerleader and supporter through everything and encouraging me for years to publish my poetry in a book! Well, hey Ma, it took me forever, but hey, here we are, I did it! And I couldn't have come this far without you!

I'd also like to thank my father, Chuck, for always being my rock and being there for me and being a great artistic teacher and role model and always pushing me to exceed my own expectations and push the boundaries I've set on myself and showing me there are no limits, and that you're never too old 😄.

My stepfather, Rich, for loving and accepting me just as I am and never trying to change me even when you don't have to.

I have SO many teachers I'd like to thank, Mr. Saterlee, Ms. Thouin, Mrs. Lavick, Mrs. Spence, Mrs. Ramsay, Ms. Cahill, Mr. Snyder, Dan and Janelle from the New School, and Mr. Yao and Mr. Martin my psychology professors. Special thank you to Ms. Cahill and Mr. Snyder for really guiding, encouraging, and pushing me with my poetry. I appreciate each and every one of you SO much.

I'd like to thank my boyfriend who has put up with me talking about doing this for years and FINALLY doing it, and all my crazy ideas and post it notes all over the house, listening to me read something I wrote, bouncing ideas off him and asking for feedback, etc. You've been amazing through this babe, thank you!

To my grandparents: My Mema and Grandpa V, you've always had my back and I love and appreciate you so much! I'd truly never be to this point without you!

To my (step) children: I love the three of you so much! You have been a source of inspiration for so much of my art! Never be afraid to follow your dreams, be creative, and reach for the stars! You can achieve anything!

To my counselor: It took me many years to give counseling a shot, and a few more to finally find someone I can trust, and absolutely amazing counselor that has my back, but also calls me out when I need it, and has listened to me without judgement for quite some time now. You have also been my cheerleader and great supporter through this journey. I am forever grateful for you. Thank you!

To Daysha: Thank you so much girl! I've only been here a little over 6 months and I can't tell you how much I appreciate you! Thank you for supporting me with this, listening to me, relighting my poetic spark, & inspiring my poem 😊

And also, to my new boss, Debbie! She doesn't even know it (well, she does now if she's reading this haha) but she was the one that got me to the point of just go for it and actually put this in motion! She also helped me land on this title 😊 She's the best!

Table of Contents:

1. I See You Everywhere
2. The Unknown
3. Betrayed Goddess
4. A Life Not Worth Living
5. Hate to Love Me
6. Through a Soldier's Eyes
7. Untamed Flame
8. I Can't Adult Today
9. Rio de Janeiro
10. I Lost My Flame
11. White Bliss
12. He Sips
13. Hello
14. Pass on By...
15. The Haunting
16. The Voyage
17. For You – I Will
18. All the Things I Should Have Said in Counseling
19. You Were Never Mine
20. Falling for You
21. Daddy's Here
22. Forever Mine
23. War Within
24. Victim of the Shadows
25. Stay
26. What If?
27. Non-Existence
28. Under
29. Cold Blooded Innocence
30. On Sanity's Edge
31. Maple Syrup & Wooden Wonders
32. What's at Stake
33. Whiskey Pulled the Trigger
34. Amora, My Love
35. Dear Grandfather
36. PuRe ChAoS
37. Hi, My Name Is...

"Rooted"
By Aminika Lee 2020

I See You Everywhere

When I look in your eyes,

I see wisdom.

When I look at your face,

I see happiness.

When I look at you,

I see me.

When I close my eyes to sleep,

I see you.

When I dream,

I dream of you.

So tell me,

Are you just a dream?

Some say I'm crazy.

Some say I'm weird.

Some say they believe in spirits and that's what you are…

But you're not just a spirit.

You're real.

Because I see you everywhere;

I see you everywhere.

The Unknown

Eastern white pine trees scrape the inky moonlit sky,
A cool, damp bed of witch hobble and honeysuckle
blends with ferns and mosses
That cushion my feet on the forest floor.
Scents of balsam fir and pine tickle my nose
As they rush in with the chill autumn Adirondack breeze
 brushing across my face.
Only the moon illuminates the path
as far as my eyes can see,
Casting a soft milky golden glow as it reflects off the leaves.
I know these woods; they're mapped out for me
Through the blood in my veins
I find my peace here –
In the stillness of the night, the forest and I come to life.
Ancestors to my left and right
They walk along beside me.
My future is unknown, but no longer am I afraid.
I have become one with those who have come before me
And push forward on the unbeaten path,
Into the unknown,
I create my own road.

Betrayed Goddess

Her body – porcelain, soft & smooth.
Looked that of a goddess, curvy and sweet
Her hair – bright, bouncy curls
Kissed by the sun
Lips of an angel
Heart of gold.
Delicate.
Innocent and pure.
It stung her skin
As though she cried acid
Her tears streamed to the floor
Pinned down
She put up the fight of her life
But the thrusts upon her were too strong
She fought with all her might
She screamed, piercing and loud
Yet, completely silent
How is it that no one heard her desperate cries for help?
The agonizing invasion
Never seemed to stop.
She hid within herself
Her body covered in scars.
Faster and deeper
She grew numb
And collapsed to the floor.
Her wings – broken
Snaped so she can no longer fly.
The thrusts continue
She tries to crawl away
But a swift kick to the back of her knees keeps her at bay
And she's dragged back to the ruthless invasion.
Repeatedly.
She has fallen,
Betrayed… helpless.
The life leaves her eyes
And all innocence disappears.

A Life not Worth Living

I was made from harsh labor,
Made carelessly, no love in my creation.
Born in a factory, among millions of brothers and sisters
I will never see again.
They hurt me,
Fill me to my physical extent with poison after poison.
Once my birth process is over
I am stuffed into a dark, cold carton
Surrounded and pushed close to 19 other siblings
Though we will soon die.
We go on a journey, shipped out around the globe
Where we are stacked on shelves and wait, frightened,
Knowing the end is to come.
My pack is bought, I feel pressure and coldness
As I am stripped away from my family.
I am lit.
It burns, I cry as my last burst of life
Sparks to its end.
More poisons are created, and I die
Also slowly killing all those surrounding me.
I am thrown to the cold, wet ground
Stomped on
And I die
A life not worth living.

Hate to Love Me

What is it about me?
My deep, mysterious, baby blue eyes?
Or, perhaps it's my kind, warm, inviting smile?
Maybe it's my confident, well-poised walk
And the bounce of my hair?
Is it the sweet, sassy way my hips sway
When I walk to a rhythm
All my own?
No?
Is my beauty appealing?
Does my sexiness offend you?
Perhaps it's the way I present myself
Soft, shy, and sweet...yet
Confident, outgoing, and ambitious?
Do I confuse you?
Yes?
Good, because I confuse myself.
Don't bother with the attempt to "figure me out",
You won't, I am a woman
And you'll just waste your time.
Don't bother.
Is it my way with words?
Or, just maybe, it's my wittiness?
Is it how I am always so uplifting and encouraging?
Maybe it's the fact that
I can hold my own?
I don't need a man.
Does the mysteriousness about me
Lure you in?
Is it the way I speak in riddles?
So often seeming so wise,
Making you come up with the answers
To the very questions you ask.
Do I come across to you as a puzzle
That you just can't put together?
Is there a piece or two missing?

Do I intrigue you?
Do you feel graced in my presence?
Perhaps?
Is it the smooth, silkiness of my hair?
Or the way it curls?
Maybe it's the soft warmth of my skin?
Is it the gentle sleekness of my lips?
Or the mint, coolness of my breath?
What is it that draws you to me?
The calming feel of my soothing touch?
Well?
No matter…
Either way
You still love me so.

Through a Soldier's Eyes

Over the sound of gunfire
Through the lifeless smoke
On the soils of a foreign country
We fear the words our commander spoke.
The air around me
Thick as blood.
The colorless souls
They seem to flood.
In the far distance
I see a face,
But then she's gone
Without a trace.
"Fight for your country!"
That's what I've been told.
She stands before me
Her colors so true and bold,
Majestically waving high
As they touch
The smoldering sky.

Untamed Flame

She's not like the others –
The path she walks she paves herself
Guided by ancestors and
The gods of the old ways.
She climbs to mountain tops
And shouts Oðin's praise.
She starts her mornings off
With runs with Tyr.
When it storms
She dances and pours a drink for Thor.
In the moonlight she casts runes
And awakens the skies.
There is a fierce fire that
Burns bright within her.
She's not like the others -
She is a flame that cannot be tamed.

I Can't Adult Today

I can't adult today.
I got up out of bed, and yes,
I am physically awake, but my mind is asleep
I'm exhausted.
My brain is mush.
I can't focus long enough to even process a thought,
But I've got 200 emails and a stack of papers
On my desk I must get through by noon
But I'm tired! I'm just so tired.
My body aches and I couldn't sleep
My mind wouldn't stop worrying about all the
Things I need to get done & how.
I'm so burnt out
I can't adult today.
I'm on my second cup of coffee and it's
Only 9AM
But without the caffeine I start to fall asleep
And this report isn't gonna write itself!
The phones ring – call after call, I can't keep up
With them all
And now my cell phones ringing too
The caller I.D. shows that it's my kid's school...
He's throwing up
And due to COVID guidelines he's gotta get picked up
My daughter too 'cause they live under the same roof
Quarantine.
It's only 10:30AM; I have so much work left to do
But now I gotta leave and find a way to get my kids from school
And to the doctor
My boss is pissed – now I'll be out for 14 days – she tells me
I need to make the tough decision, it's the kids or my job
Wait, what?
I can't adult today.
So now I'm on the bus on my way to my kid's school

Minds racing and I'm trying to call the doctor but nobody's picking up
I'm a mess
I'm running through my head a new list of all I need to do
I'm so stressed, and now there's pains in my chest
I gotta just ignore it all and continue pushing through
I gotta pick up groceries and run to the pharmacy too
To ensure we have all we need to get us through this quarantine
All of this and it's not even yet noon
I can't adult today.
I just need a helping hand
Someone to help take a little off my plate
Just for a minute so I can have a break
For a moment, catch my breath,
Rebuild my strength
Before it's back to the home schooling, back to remotely working
Back to the laundry, the dishes, the cleaning, and the cooking
It's too much!
I feel like the weight of the worlds on my shoulders
And I'm caving under the pressure
I have no time to myself
And now, my boss is demanding me to be at work full-time
When the kids are home from school in quarantine,
And I don't understand
Why she's always gotta pick on me, she doesn't
Do this shit to anybody else
I'm going crazy
I can't find a babysitter and I've got less than 24 hours' notice
Because after today I'm not allowed to work remotely like everybody else
Everything's happening so fast, and my boss is
Being so bitter
I don't know what I ever did to her
But I know I don't deserve the way she treats me
This is crazy!
Is it 4:30 yet?
I can't adult today.

Rio de Janeiro

I will go to Rio
I will dress as a Flamingo
I will drive in my chevy truck
That feels excited and anxious to go
I will go to Rio
Drive through the roads of America's states
To the hot border of México
Past Venezuela
I will go to Rio
I will pass the Amazon
Where the trees feel like butterflies
Fluttering about above
The monkeys fly and sing as birds
Up high in the swaying trees
Where the macaws are vibrant like rainbows
I will go to Rio
Where it smells of excitement, dance, sweat, salt water
Food, parties, and night life
The bars reek of alcohol and sex
I will go to Rio
Where the fruit is the sweetest
Down to the seed
I will eat the most pleasurable fruits
Ah, the delightful taste of Acai berries
Where I will eat Feijoada
And I will drink Caipirinha
I will dance on
Into the whispering night
I will go to Rio
I will sit on the beach
And embrace the silver ocean's shimmer
As the water salsas with my toes
And the heat caresses me
And gently rocks me to sleep
Where the sun kisses my skin
Leaving it a beautiful golden brown
I will go to Rio
I will go back home

I will lie in the sea
And drift away like a feather
I will go to Rio
To where the birds, the trees, the sea
Speak my language
Where the people are warm and kind
And familia vem em prinerio lugar (family comes first)
And the grass is soft and sweet
Greener then the flag
Or any of the ripest limes
I will go to Rio
I will go back home

I Lost My Flame

Hey... it's me.
Umm, I just wanted to give you a call
To hear your voice again...
Silly, I know, but, I still have so much
I need to say
Uhg... this just, can't be real...
I know I'm a day too late but okay, here it goes...
Remember all the nights we'd spend just walkin' round for hours?
We'd talk, we'd sing, we'd stop & smell the flowers
And you'd always pick one
And put it in my hair and we'd silently fall a little harder.
You were right there
Always to catch me when I'd fall
And you were right there
Always my biggest cheerleader, man we made it through it all
Every up, every down
We were inseparable
We'd always go through it all together
Always thought you'd be my forever
Never thought I'd see a day
Where you'd be gone, and I'd be left here, alone
I should have told you...
I should have told you that for so long
I hid feelings for you that were so strong
I just didn't want to risk it all, couldn't have anything go wrong – no chance
I didn't want to take a chance that I may ruin what we had
And scare you away
But fuck it, you're away now and you
Ain't comin' back, man I'm broken

I just want you to know that I'm sorry...
I'm sorry that it took me so long to say
What I should have said all along
I love you
And I have since practically day one
I wish that our story didn't end like this
I always thought that one day
I'd be your wife and we'd have a real nice life
Together
Not like this... it wasn't supposed to be like this.
Now I'm bringing flowers to lay by your head – your name in stone
I can't do this...
I can't go on and pretend that I'm okay
I can't go on alone, I lost the twin to my flame the day
That yours went out, but hey
Do me one last favor okay? Please never leave me
I feel you.
Though you may not be on this same earth plane with me now
Just know, my love for you is forever; it will never grow cold, it'll never die out –
Forever.
Forever is what we always said
"Best friends forever"
So, I'll carry that with me,
I'll carry *you* with me
Until the day I pass away too and together
We will be once more, together
A ghost love for all of eternity
I love you
Forever.
Forever can't come too soon.

"Blossoms In Bloom"

By Aminika Lee

May 2022

White Bliss

A blissful chill in the air
Awakens the heavy grey clouds
They stretch and yawn
As I slip out.

My journey begins
I flutter about
Each gentle breeze
Carries me closer to the earth

What a pretty sight
Tree tops blanketed in white
Sweet, warm fire light blissfully flickering
From the windows you can see five Christmas stockings

Frozen ponds etched with figure eights
Children build snowmen
With their tongues in the air
Begging to catch a simple flake

I drift and sway
In every which way
While the children lay
Silently, eagerly awaiting the man in red.

Gifts wrapped under a tree
Topped with a star
Milk and cookies
Half-eaten on the table

Back up through the chimney
Off on to the next house
On the roof, I await him
For I have landed on his sleigh

On into the night
Into the mystic white bliss
My journey begins again
As the Mrs. awaits her Christmas kiss.

He Sips

When she talks
He can feel it burn.
The poison dripping off her lips,
Every word driving him one step closer.
That bottle pressed up against his lips,
The people called him the "town drunk"
What they didn't know was
That she was his drug.
Eyes red – blood shot
Sip by sip
He succumbs to the power
He slips deeper and deeper
As her lips drip, drip –
And he sips.
Trying to kill the pain
And the demons that have taken him over
She lied.
He cries.
The bottle at his lips
Might as well pull the trigger,
It'll destroy his life just the same.
She's got it all
And he's got nothing left, no pride.
He hides, buried in the bottle
Nothing left to live for.
He's focused on her,
She's catastrophic –
He's blind.
How can't he see?
The miracles they created
Are still a part of his life
Nothing can take them away.
But he sees his life as over – washed up.
Dark.
Everything fades to shades of grey.
As he sips, he slips
Into a place so dark
He thinks there's no coming back,
Demons take control.

His heads spinning
But wait,
A faint light
Something pulling him back
A voice.
Giving him meaning again.
"Daddy!"
He hears his name
But still, it's not enough.
He sips.

Hello

Hello?
Can you hear me?
Hello?
I'm here, trapped inside!
Hello?
I can't escape, buried in my mind!
Hello?
Please, someone help me!
Hello?
Do you have the key?
Hello?
Help! She's eating me alive!
Hello?
I beg you, help, I can't break free!
Hello?
Please help, I am my own worst enemy!
Hello?
Is anyone there?
Hello?
Hello...
Please, rescue me!

Pass on By...

I have a family
But, how would you know?
Day by day you mindlessly walk by me
Different day, same routine
I doubt you even notice me.
Every day, I see the same thing
Same people going to the same places
Their phones pressed up to their absent faces
Robotic.
Same path, same route
Same coffee order.
All in such a rush.
What a hurried world we live in.
"Homeless".
It's almost as though I am a ghost
Drifting away at sea
The sea full of people
I'm surrounded, but you look right through me.
I have a story.
You see here, this scar is from an accident I had in training
I almost didn't complete, but I'm not one to let something
Silly like that keep me down.
And yes, half my arm is missing
Ya see, back in 1973... it was ruff in 'Nam
Jimmy tried to push me out the way
But he was a moment too late.
I have a wife.
My beautiful Mary-Ann.
Her smile alone could light up any room
Oh, you should have seen her on our wedding day,
I've never seen anything more beautiful.
It was 1982
We danced. Oh, how she loved to dance and glide across
the room.

You should have seen her...
And my daughter! Ah, yes, two years later my Mary-Ann blessed me
With my sweet, sweet Katie-Lynn.
She had curls. The most bouncy, golden curls
That whirled as she twirled around
She loved to dance, just like her mother...
It was October
Of 2004, my sweet Katie was in labor
For hours, it was excruciating, but she put up a fight
Now I have my granddaughter to raise, Mary-Kate...
But I lost my sweet Katie at just 22
Man, time flies...
I spent all I could to get Mary-Kate into her dream school
She wants to be a doctor.
My sweet girl wants to help save the world.
Ah, time flies.
I can't believe she's already grown.
18 now, all in the blink of an eye
Time flies.
Enjoy it. Listen to the stories.
Cherish it.
    I have a story.
    But, how would you know?

The Haunting

Come to sleep
Don't let me lay here alone
I know I push you away but I love it when you're close
All the feelings you awake in me
Paralyzed, I lose all mobility
          The darkness sets in
          My senses tingling
          This is where the haunting begins.
Like a wave, it takes over me
Crashing, pulling me in, a sweet caress from which I can't break free!
Trembling, the images appear, I see
Everything unfolds so vividly
          The darkness digs within
          My emotions run paper thin
          This is where my haunting begins.
I can feel it as I fade away
Trapping me, ensuring that there will be no escape!
I cannot run, I fall to my knees
As the tears fall steadily
Acid burning my cheeks
There's nowhere to escape, I quickly slip away
Vision starts to fade, I cry but no one can hear my pain
Fallen numb, I succumb to the blade
Someone won't you rescue me?
          The darkness from within
          The cuts on my skin
          This is where my haunting begins.
Please save me?
Won't you drag me to the light?
Breathe me back to life!
Please save me!
 Please, take my hand
Don't let me go
Don't let it take me!
No! Please save me!
          The darkness settled in
          My cold, pale skin
          This is where my haunting begins.
You were too late.

"Smoldering Seas"
By: Aminika Galusha
April, 2022

THE VOYAGE

Ships set sail on treacherous waters
Shields lined down the vessel's side
Beneath the hull, the sea's filled with horrors
Depths unknown, exploring blind.
Waves are crashing, tossing & turning
Below the planks, weapons grind.
The skies above, clouds are raging
With Njörd, our fates entwined!
Bursts of thunder & strikes of lightning
Pouring rain, making us near-blind!
Our journey ahead can prove to be frightening
But Thor will guide us home!
(Oooh oh oh oh)
We live to tell our story
(Oooh oh oh oh)
With Tyr as our guide, we thrive for victory!
(Oooh oh oh oh)
We live our lives honorably
(Oooh oh oh oh)
All for Odin's glory!

FOR YOU – I WILL

For you, I will get out of bed each morning
Put a smile on my face & comb my hair.
For you I will never give up
Try a little harder, push a little further
For you I will hold my head a little higher
And talk about myself a bit sweeter
For you I will learn to live life
And not just take it for a passing moment —
Time is something we can never get back & no longer
Will I take it for granted.
For you I will keep holding on, even when I want to give up
And throw in my flag.
For you I will open my heart wider & love a little deeper.
For you I will carry the burdens of the world on my shoulders
And pull you through
For you, I will survive & be thankful to be alive
      For you, I will.

All the Things I Should Have Said in Counseling

Hello, Aminika – how are you?
I'm not too bad, and yourself?
Good, good. How's everything going?
Not too bad. Works been fine; I guess it gets a little stressful on some days.
But overall, fine.
Good to hear. Sounds like things are getting better. Sorry to hear it can get stressful; that happens at times with jobs. Just keep up with your coping skills and do your grounding exercises if ever the stress becomes too much.
And remember – you've got this!
How's home?
Eh, ya know... good. Surviving. Getting by day to day – it could be worse.
That's good, sometimes that's all you can do, just relax, don't stress, and take life day to day.
... ...
Okay Aminika, that's time.
Anything else before I let you go?
Umm... no. I'm good.
Thank you – see you next week.
You're welcome, see you next week.
Take care of yourself.
Thanks, you too. Bye!
Bye.
...
But wait... there's more.
I lied, I'm not okay.
Work has me super stressed
And leaves me burnt out at the end of each day.
I can't take it.
My boss is always picking me apart and
Comparing me to others and

She's always so rude – doing all she can to
Make me feel inadequate and not valued.
And the workloads never stop
Requests keep coming in and piling up
We're behind and understaffed
At this pace we can't keep up.
It's a high stress environment.
Tension fills the air – everyone's on edge
It's toxic.
So I keep my mouth shut and
On eggshells I walk.
This is crazy – this isn't healthy
I should quit!
But I really need this job
So I stay and push on through
She even made me choose
Between my family or my job.
This is insane!
Sure, the kids technically aren't mine
But who is she to say?!
They live with me and for the last 5 years
I've been the mother-figure in their lives and
Their main source of support – it's all on me!
And I love and care for them as though they were my own
It makes no difference, honestly
It's not her place to say!
Who is she to make me choose?!
This is bullshit!
I've tried to reach out for help but it all leads
Back to her
What more can I do?
I dream of leaving…
And at home
No, it's not okay
We're actually really struggling
I can't make ends meet –
Bills keep piling up, rent is due

The kitchen's empty and I don't know how I'm affording food
I'm drowning.
It's just me working.
Everyone expects me to be superhuman
But I am just me, I'm just a person!
But I've got a family at home
And they all rely on me to provide
And have all the answers
So, I cannot break – I've got to be strong
But the pressure is on
Truth be told I'm breaking...
But I suffer silently
So, they do not see
How often I lock myself alone in a room
And break down
I cry and beg myself to stop
I squeeze my arms around my chest to try to hold myself together
Pieces of me are falling as I
Scream at myself in the mirror
To wipe away those tears, pick myself up off the floor
Get it together!
Gotta be stronger –
But these thoughts run wild in my mind
I'm thinking about ending my life
And all the different ways to do it –
How to make it easier for whoever finds me and how
To make absolute sure that *that* "whoever" is **not** the kids
I cry harder.
I do not want to die.
But I cannot take all of the pressures that come
With trying to stay alive
Am I even strong enough to escape suicide?
I haven't even begun to scratch the surface
Of everything that's bothering me...
It's so much – from work, at home, relationships, and such things to

The larger scale and global crisis
Yeah, that shits scary!
Plus, the depression that I've been feeling from things
Regarding my hopes and dreams... for example
I'd like to travel.
I'd like to explore
Get out there and see the world!
And I'd like a house.
I thought that by now at this point in my life
I'd at least be close and have a decent savings
To buy a house.
A place I can really make my own
And call home – and marriage...
I always thought that I'd be married around 30, at least engaged.
For sure, I thought I'd be engaged by now at this point in my life
I'm a good woman.
I have a good job, I'm loyal, I provide, I love deeper than the sea...
It's been years now that we've been together
But no signs are pointing in that direction...
I don't understand...
I'm a very good woman, I know that...
What am I doing wrong?
I feel heavy.
Uhg! I've gained so much weight
I feel gross.
I don't like who I see in the mirror
On top of being concerned for my health
I feel heavy...
Mentally I'm really struggling right now.
And the worst part is
I can't even figure out how to tell you how I feel
Because it's too much!
It's overwhelming, I can't even find the right words.
And to add to that I don't even know where to start

I want to release all of these emotions
But I can't even get the emotions to come out
Which just causes more stress and frustration!
I'm thrown into this vicious cycle with no end,
At times, I legitimately don't even know what I'm feeling
Or why... what's the trigger?
And that's a scary feeling all in itself – not knowing.
What's gonna happen in the future?
I know. I know what you're going to say
Tellin' me not to stress about the tomorrows and just
Live presently for today
But today fuckin sucks!
I just need something to look forward to!
Please tell me that it's going to be okay
Because my yesterdays don't paint a pretty picture
They've given me so much pain...
The pain - don't even get me started on the pain
I know we've been seeing one another for a while now
But that's not something we get to touch on a lot
And I know it's been years –
I promise I've been trying to deal, trying to heal
But it still hurts.
The memories and the dreams keep flashing back,
They keep me up at night
I cannot sleep, it's like a fuckin curse
But what in the hell did I ever do to deserve this
I was a kid!
I was just a kid and I was raped of my innocence
In every meaning of the word
Why!?
Why would anyone do that to another at all, especially more than once?
Then claim the next day they love you?!
I can't wrap my head around it.
I try so hard not to torture myself, but I can't help but wonder
What the hell was going through his mind every time
And what was he thinking

Every time he'd destroy our home or
Lay his hands on my mother?!
Why!?
Why did he have so much hate in his heart?
Why'd he want to hurt us so bad
Again, and again and again
He must be mad…. Right?
Surely – he must be out of his mind…
But the worst part is – there was also good times!
Amusement parks, road trips & fancy cars – dancing and shopping!
I hate to remember this monster, my abuser, as fun!
How could he be fun?!
The more that I think the more that I drive myself insane
I wish it could all just go away
But no matter what I do it's always on replay at night!
I'm scared to dream – he haunts me there.
I just want to be at peace!
But wait – there's so much more I never say
Like how lonely I am or how I am afraid to get close to anyone
I'm "so young" yet all of my best friends are dead, all but one – and she moved away
And until now I've never said how much it bothers me
But it does… or
How bad I've been at adjusting to her being gone,
But man, I've been really struggling with it
Way more than I'd care to admit
But I'm happy for her, she's doing alright
I just struggle with talking to her now
And I don't know why
I just feel like a burden,
Like I'm a bother…
But I miss her so much!
I miss them all.
I wish there was calling hours for
the loved ones we've lost
I've never felt more alone…

My dogs my best friend.
She's my everything, although,
While we're on the topic and I'm admitting things
I guess I should confess
That I haven't been taking Amora's passing very well –
It's been months.
She was truly my everything.
When I reached out for a hand,
She found me and gave me her paw
I just can't cope...
It really hurts.
I've been trying to "stay strong" and lean on
My other dog, Shenzi, she's the best
Such a good, sweet girl
She's taught me so much.
I love her dearly,
But I'm still hurting.
I feel like such a mess!
Shit, I can't even afford these therapy appointments
My bills racking up –
Which is stressful.
Ironic – isn't that?
But I need you,
So, I'll figure something out... right?
Sure, I always do...
But it seems all my options have finally run out
I feel so heavy.
I'm not sure I can keep going on.
But enough already, I've blabbed your ear off
Yet didn't even scrape the surface
Of everything that's torturing my mind
And all the things that I should have said in counseling.

You Were Never Mine

Just when I thought I had you
Just when I thought you were mine
Just when I thought you loved me
You & I 'til the end of time.
There you go again
Fading away like a dream
So I grab a pen
Try to put us into ink
Before it's too late
And you're just a mere memory.
I swear I loved you
But I guess it didn't show?
You're so far gone
And I'm wishin' we could just go back home
Back to how we were
Back to us
The smiles, the laughs, the love
But I guess it was just never enough.

Falling for You

Many years have come and gone
Miserable past relationships that dragged on and on.
This time around is different, my dear
I'm falling for you without a fear.

Your eyes, so pure,
Dripping emotions sweet as honey
Deep and full of life, they draw me in.
Drifting away in their alluring mystery.

The words rolling off your lips
Everything I've always needed to hear.
What I was so once blinded to
I now see crystal clear.

The touch of your skin
Sets me into a trance
A state most pure – relaxation.
A world all our own.

The taste of your lips
Like marvelous sugar cane
A candy made solely for my addiction,
Luscious and sweet.

Now I know this may sound crazy, darlin'
But I'm falling for you
And I've no idea how else to put this –
I love you.

Daddy's Here

Standing in the delivery room
The doctor hands me a pink bundle with eyes -- light blue
She yawns, stretches, and opens her eyes.
I knew right then and there
That my whole world had changed
Looking at the face of my baby girl
Nothing would ever be the same

And at the moment that I first heard her cry
She became the top priority in my life,
I was her protector,
As I took her in my arms I said

Stop you're crying
Baby, wipe them tears.
No more worries, princess Daddy's here;
To fight away all of your fears
And shine some light in your atmosphere.
I'll put the sun up to brighten your day
And I'll place the moon to guide your way.
So, no more worries, baby, wipe them tears,
Daddy's here.

I blink my eyes and suddenly my little girl
Is in high school and outgrew her curls
And she comes to me and say's
"Daddy, I got asked to go to the Prom!"
It's a boy from here in town,
Her mama nearly broke down,
Our little girl has grown up so fast.
She asks for my opinion on her dress
I tell her she looks beautiful, kiss her head
And send her on her way.

She comes home crying one night,
Says "Daddy, he broke my heart".
I wrap her in my arms
And hold her tight and softly say

Stop you're crying
Baby, wipe them tears.
No more worries, princess Daddy's here;
To fight away all of your fears
And shine some light in your atmosphere.
I'll put the sun up to brighten your day
And I'll place the moon to guide your way.
So, no more worries, baby, wipe them tears,
Daddy's here.

I blink again, and she's fully grown.
Hell, she's even got two kids of her own,
And a husband that loves her so dear.
I'm lyin' in the hospital bed
She's sittin' at my side and kisses my head,
She's got tears built up in her eyes.
I tell her be strong and not to cry, this isn't goodbye
Just a, see you when I see you.
I rest my hand on her knee,
She turns her head and looks all glossy-eyed at me,
And I whisper

Stop you're crying
Baby, wipe them tears.
No more worries, **princess Daddy's here;**

To fight away all of your fears
And shine some light in your atmosphere.
I'll put the sun up to brighten your day
And I'll place the moon to guide your way.
So, no more worries, baby, wipe them tears,
Daddy's here.
Daddy's always right here.

Forever Mine

Melting, my heart forms a pool
Of such warm, inviting, vibrant light.
My eyes beam when I look at you,
My knees grow weak,
And suddenly all I see is you & me.
I don't know what it is about you –
Your smile?
Or, maybe it's that deep, loving, protective look in your eye?
I'm not sure baby, but I'm in love with you just the same.
Day by day you warm my heart,
You melt my soul & break the ice,
Bringing me to life.
Your tender kiss upon my lips,
Breathing me into a new light.
We're in a world
Made for just us two.
Breathless, I wrap my arms around you,
Taking you all in.
Silently, I pray
That nothing will ever take you away
I hold you close
Wishing for this to never end
And for you to be
Forever mine.

War Within

I've been trying to escape it
The feeling of being anxious and lonely.
That feeling of feeling nauseous every time I turn out the lights
That feeling of immobilizing fear when I try to rest my head on a pillow
I can't sleep.
I know what's waiting for me on the other side
Every time I close my eyes
I know its weak
Of me to keep running away from my dreams
But it's not just a dream
It's my reality
I've been there, I've lived it, and it's crippling me
You can't see the demons caged within, you can't see
The battles I've fought
The paralyzing series of unfortunate events that
I've been forced to live through
I'm anxious.
I'm almost 30 and still afraid to be alone
I can't move, the fear consumes me, and I'll do nothing all day
Drowning in the silence
I won't even eat, then come night
I cannot sleep if I know that no one is home but me
I hear voices in the back of my head telling me I ain't safe
Not to close my eyes
That I will not be okay if I let my guard down
Even for a millisecond
I can't sleep.
Like ghosts in the attic, my life is haunting me.
I stare blankly at the ceiling as it takes over me
I can't speak, I want
To tell you all just exactly how I feel
I want to speak, to ask for help
I can't breathe, my throat burns
The demons pull on my vocal cords and tie them
Around my neck to make a noose

I can't speak
My voice cannot be heard
I feel crazy
Overwhelmed by all these intrusive thoughts and memories
So please forgive me if sometimes I don't want to be
Here. I constantly think about giving in, letting the demons choke me
Until I can no longer breathe,
Just let them take me.
I'm anxious. I'm afraid.
Anxiety is not something I can just exchange, it's taken up nearly 20 years of my life and I can't get it back!
I'm forced to find a solution and deal with the constant pain, I'm afraid.
I'm always told to pray; doctors say that medicine will clear the way
For me to heal
But I've tried it all and yet I'm still here,
At war with myself
There is no way out
When does it end?
Is there really even a solution
Or is it all just temporary lies to yourself to
Numb the pain for a while just so you can get a break
And build up your strength
Just so you can build up more armor and go right back in to battle
On the front line
Yet I'm bleeding out and dying inside
How do I escape?

Victim of the Shadows

There is a darkness within me
Dragging me in
Tugging on my soul
Drowning me.
I can barely put up a fight
Deeper and deeper it absorbs me
I can hardly glimpse the light
As it fades away
And I fall victim to the shadows
All I've tried to suppress
Rises to the surface and eats away
At my soul and releases
All the demons within.
The world comes crashing,
Collapsing all around
I'm drowning with my eyes wide open
I cry for help
But nobody can hear a sound
I've lost the battle & now I see
I've closed myself off trying to protect me
From those I thought would hurt me
But all I've done is lock away the one
That would ultimately destroy me,
buried deep down inside
I've lost the war ragging within
As I drown, everything goes blurry
Yet somehow, I can finally see so clearly
That all this time the enemy has been inside
Of me, now I see
I am my own worst enemy.

Stay

She has no will to live
She's fading on me
I know she loves me
But it's not enough to hold her here
The pressure keeps building up
She's going to snap, it's just too much.
I reach out and hug her
Hold her together as she cries
She doesn't want to be alive
She can't take the stress or the pain
She can't fight anymore
She wants to die
She wants to take her life

So I will fight for her
I will be her light
I'll hold her up & guide her way
She wants to die
But I'll bring her back to life
I'll be her breath in her lungs, her blood in her veins
I'll be her strength
And like a phoenix from the ashes
She will rise
I'll make her want to stay alive.

"Rising From The Flames"
Photo Credit: Aminika Galusha of
Bella Luna Photography
02/12/2022

What If...

What if I told you I still love you?
Would you think I'm crazy?
Or would you take me by the hand and call me baby
And start over again?
Try harder.
Try forever?
What if I told you I forgive you?
That although yes, you hurt me,
I still want to be with you.
That I can still envision a future for us
For our family
And I want to build a life with you.
What if I told you that, try as I may,
This isn't like past relationships
And I can't just give up and walk away –
Not from you.
What if I asked you to take my hand,
Come home with me, start anew...
Would you walk with me?
What if I told you I'm still in love with you?

Non-Existence

Do you believe in the paranormal?
Yes, you do.
For I do not exist.
I am solely a ghostly void
A mere figment of false existence.
I am not here, there is no me.
This body that you see standing before you
Is just an empty shell
Hollowed out by memories of what used to be.
There is no me.
Now close your eyes and let me slip away
Our shadows dance
And your tongue flicks words
Rolling off your lips,
Those that you can't take back
And those that you wish you had said.
As I fade into the abyss
I do not exist.
Wipe those tears away
And remove your hand from its grip on my wrist
You can't make me stay.
What did Daddy always say?
Not to cry over imaginary friends.
I am make believe.
You once believed in me, but
That does not prove that I am real
There is no me.
I do not exist!

Under

Stop telling me that
"You gotta love yourself first"
Because right now, I don't love myself
Enough to keep myself from
A final ride in the back of
a hearse.
I don't need Superman,
I just need someone to reach out their hand
And hold my head above water
Cause on my own
I'm drowning.

Cold Blooded Innocence

Why is it that we love those who hurt us,
And we hurt those who love us?
Why do we always want what we can't have?
Why do we let precious love slip away?
Why do we not try to keep our love true?
Why don't you treat me the way that I treat you?
And why is it that hearts keep beating
When so many are broken?
How can the one to save you,
Be the same one to kill you?
And how can one say words
Only meant to destroy another's heart?
Why do we build each other up,
To watch one another fall apart?
Why do we take and take,
But never give?
How can our hearts freeze?
How can we turn so cold?
How can we make others feel so incomplete?
How can we pretend not to care when the truth is,
The feelings are really there?
Why do we willingly give up our all to someone
And leave ourselves so vulnerable;
So open to pain?
Why is it that we accept the pain?
Why do we shut ourselves down?
Why are we so afraid?
Why do we hurt?
Why do we inflict pain?
Why are we put through such hell?
And why is it that, though we hurt each other,
We can't hate anymore?

On Sanity's Edge

What's the use of life
If you don't want to live?
What's the use of a heart
When your heart gets shattered
To crimson bloody pieces all around you?
What's the use of breath
When you're buried so deep within yourself--
Unable to breathe?
Suffocating?
What's the use of a soul
When you're already dead?
What's the point of a voice
When it's words you're forbidden to speak?
What's the point of feelings
When you've grown so overwhelmingly numb?
What's the point of love
If all that comes out of it is devastating disaster?
What's the point of you and me
If you're fire
And I, gasoline
And we only bring each other tears
Of undying pain?
What's the point in living this life
When I've got nothing to lose
And nothing to gain?
Standing on the edge of sanity
Teetering back and forth
Desperately trying to decode the mystery of
What's real and what's fake
It's my soul at stake
Losing my last breath
As I fall to the end
My death
My suicide

Tell me where's the point in loving you
When it's like a sword with a double edge blade?
No matter what I do, what I say
It's gonna stab me either way.
And tell me what's the point of the truth
When it's all made up of dark and deceiving lies?
What's the point in breaking my heart
When it wasn't even whole
To start with?
Now tell me what's the use of a mind
When it's so overwhelmingly silent
That I can't hear myself think
Screaming
Save me! -- --
Losing my last breath
As I fall to the end
My death
My suicide
<SAVE ME!>

Maple Syrup and Wooden Wonders

It was May when I went to visit him again.
We parked the car at the garage and walked
Hand in hand; peacefully through the woods
Past the pond, in search of my Papa's grave
It's been five years since I was here last
 I planted the Dogwood tree right above his headstone
I left a cowboy hat and horseshoe, right there on his grave
I didn't know you then.

We walk on, past the old hunting fort
Past the oak and on to the willow
Where just beyond is his grave
He rests there beneath the willow
The pond, just a few feet away
The Dogwood in full bloom
I take you by the hand and pull you
Toward my Papa's grave
Where I fall to my knees
And cry, saying allowed how much I miss him
And what I'd do just to hear his voice,
Look into his eyes, and see him looking back
Just one more time
To taste the honey suckle
Or his home-made jam
To ride alongside him on the horses
Through the woods
Picking Princess Pine to bring home to Grandma
To make wreathes with
Or, to just see him smile and sing about
As he carved some old wood into a breath-taking work of wondrous beauty

Or perhaps just to taste one last time the sweet
Sugary, gooey, sticky taste of that wonderful
Maple Syrup he made
To sit at the wooden kitchen table he had crafted
So many years ago
And sit in the bear shaped chairs
He had made to go along with it
And see him smile
As we shared maple syrup candies he'd made
Or maple syrup on warm homemade bread Grandma had baked.

You kneel down beside me and introduce yourself to my Papa
And ask him for permission
For my hand
And swear you'll always take care of me
As he would have, and be my hero, my protector
My everything
You wrap your arms around me and kiss away my tears
Grab my hands and lift me up off the ground

We hike back to the house up on the mountain's hill
Nobody's been here in years
Nobody can bear to be here when he is gone
I hunt for the old key in my deep pocket
And gently open the door
I lead you in as we wonder about
Everything just as I remembered
Pictures upon the wall
Memory lane before my eyes
Got me reminiscing on some good times
An old deer head mounted on the wall above the table
A dog's bed on the living room floor
The hole in his favorite recliner

Carefully stitched back together by the hands of Grandma
I open the door to his room
And see the bed where he lay
A picture of Grandma and I lay on the nightstand
I brush my fingers across it and cry
Wiping off the dust
You hold me and coo in my ear
Words of comfort

I take your hand and lead you out back
To the garage
I tussle with the door and finally get it open
To the left, hunting guns and fishing poles hang on the wall
To my right, power tools and a lunch box
Before me, his work bench
A carving of his favorite dog lay there
Nearly complete, but not quite
Never did he get the chance to finish
I grab his carving knife and old chisel
You sit beside me and say, "Do you know what you're doing, love?"
I just simply reply "I've seen him do it enough"
And I carve and chisel away for hours
Its dark out
I've completed the carving

Wood
Tender, beautiful wood of wonder
My Papa made you into works of art
My Papa, a sculptor

You kiss my forehead and grab my hand
You lead me out and shut off the light
But just as we're about to walk away

The moonlight shines through the window
A jar, glistens in its glorious light
What's this?
Syrup? – Maple Syrup?
In the most beautiful jar, syrup that
My grandfather made nearly ten years ago
For his last time

I remember playing out in the field
And feeding the horses apples and sugar cubes
As Papa would walk in from the woods
A wooden yoke lay across his shoulders
Two silver buckets of sap
Hung from each side
I'd run to him
Eager to help
Make his delicious sticky sweet treat
Maple syrup
My Papa's maple syrup

We take the jar and the carving
And hike back to his grave
Out, past the barn, past the meadow, past the pond
Under that old willow
I kneel down
And place the carving of Shadow
Just beside his headstone
Beneath the Dogwood Tree
You open the jar for me
We dip our fingers in and taste it
We smile, all sticky
You kiss me, your lips, sweet like sugar
Taste of my Papa's sweetness
I dip my fingers in

And slap down and smear some sticky goodness
On the grass where his head should be
Resting
Six feet under the earth
For the syrup
To seep through to Papa's mouth
To his tongue
To taste his sweet creation one more time
And smile

Mmm, syrup
Maple Syrup
My Papa's sweet, sticky, gooey Maple Syrup

What's At Stake?

The pressure is on
The weight of the world is on my shoulders.
Got to be the best,
Be all that I can be.
Got to stay strong,
Be everything they expect of me.
Put that "S" on my chest --
But what's the point in trying to be the hero
When it's your own life at stake?

    Who's gonna save me now?

Whiskey Pulled the Trigger (Sestina form poem)

The house creaks in the dead of the night,
She lies awake silently in her bed,
Her eyes are bright red, face soaked with tears,
Grasping onto his picture
She sips down one last glass of whiskey,
Lifts her clenched, shaking hand up to her head and pulls the trigger.

Azrael* stands at her side; he lifts her hand from the trigger
No one knew the inner fight and darkness she fell into that night,
Broken glass and spilt whiskey
Covered the floor beside her bed,
Clenched in her hand was a dried out rose, lying over her heart was his picture,
Her pillow stained with her crimson tears

His eyes flooded the house with tears,
He couldn't believe she pulled the trigger.
He used his finger and traced her face in their picture,
Reminiscing about good times and the promises he vowed that night.
He sat up all night in his bed,
Trying to erase her memory with whiskey.

Glass after glass of whiskey
He just couldn't stop the tears,
He couldn't take being alone without her that night in bed.
He blamed himself for her pulling the trigger
On that stormy, dark, deadly night,
He clung on for dear life to their picture.

Knowing all he had left were memories and pictures
He drank himself through glass after glass of whiskey,
One for every year they had been married...but that night
He cried his last tears.

He opened the closet, grabbed her old riffle, laid down, put it to his chest and pulled the trigger,
A blood-pool replaced where what should have been his bed -- --

They laid them to rest in the same bed
And had engraved in their stone their picture.
A sorrowful gathering because two people pulled the trigger,
As they all toasted to their lives with a shot of whiskey
And flooded the cemetery in tears
Because of that night.

When they were up all night in their beds
Crying bloody tears and painful memories, clinging on to a picture
They couldn't get drunk enough to rid the pain and free their minds, so whiskey pulled the trigger.

*Azrael: Angel of death

Amora, My Love!

I found you at your worst
Picked you up & carried you home.
I ran you a warm bath
Washed you up & dressed your wounds.
I cooked you a big, hot meal –
Anything I had that you you'd like;
    Chicken, beef, a little egg, cheese, and carrots…
You were so fragile & weak
But you ate!
I could see the fight in your sweet eyes
You weren't ready to die!
I know Mom might
Be a little mad, but,
I was already in love
With you
And planning all I needed to do
To get you healthy and keep you safe.
The vets told me to put you down & out
Of your misery
That you wouldn't survive and
You would be a "bad dog"; vicious and mean…
No, fuck that! You were coming back home with me,
Home. Yes, home for now with me you have a new home –
Food, toys, a new bed
Love.
Love is what you needed!
Love & a chance! You are not a "bad dog"!
You never were and you'll never be a "bad dog"!
They told me you were used for
Breeding then used as bait in dog fights
But somehow, you escaped!
They kept telling me how you'd never be
Good for me & how vicious you would be, that you'd "turn"
on me
But they didn't give you a chance
All it took was just a few minutes to let you warm up
And they would have seen there was never a vicious bone in
your body!
You were so sweet, and scared at first but,

You wanted to trust people
And, even scared, you never once tried to hurt me!
So yes, you came back home with me!
As time passed and you healed, your personality really shined!
You were so sweet – gentle, patient and kind!
Everyone that met you, loved you
YOU were LOVE
Unconditional love
That's all you knew
Both how to give, and from me to you
You quickly and effortlessly became my best friend
My trusty adventure sidekick and my life partner
We did everything together!
Hikes, car rides, shopping trips… you name it.
You were always at my side.
You were with me through it all… every home, my every job, every relationship of my life right up to this point (LOL so this better be my last, babe!)
You got me through my darkest of times and
You really showed me the definition of true, undying, unconditional love.
For the longest time, I thought it was I who was saving you…
But, clear as day, anyone could see
It was actually you that saved me.
You gave me the best ten years of my life
And were truly the most kind, gentle, precious soul!
You meant the absolute world to me
Which is why, when it came time for our final farewell on this earth plane…
A huge part of me died right along with you.
Sad and heartbroken as I may be,
I refuse to believe that
You're gone.
I know you're still with me
Guiding me through
Patiently waiting
Until I find my way back to you

Mommy loves you forever & always,
    See you when I see you, my babygirl!

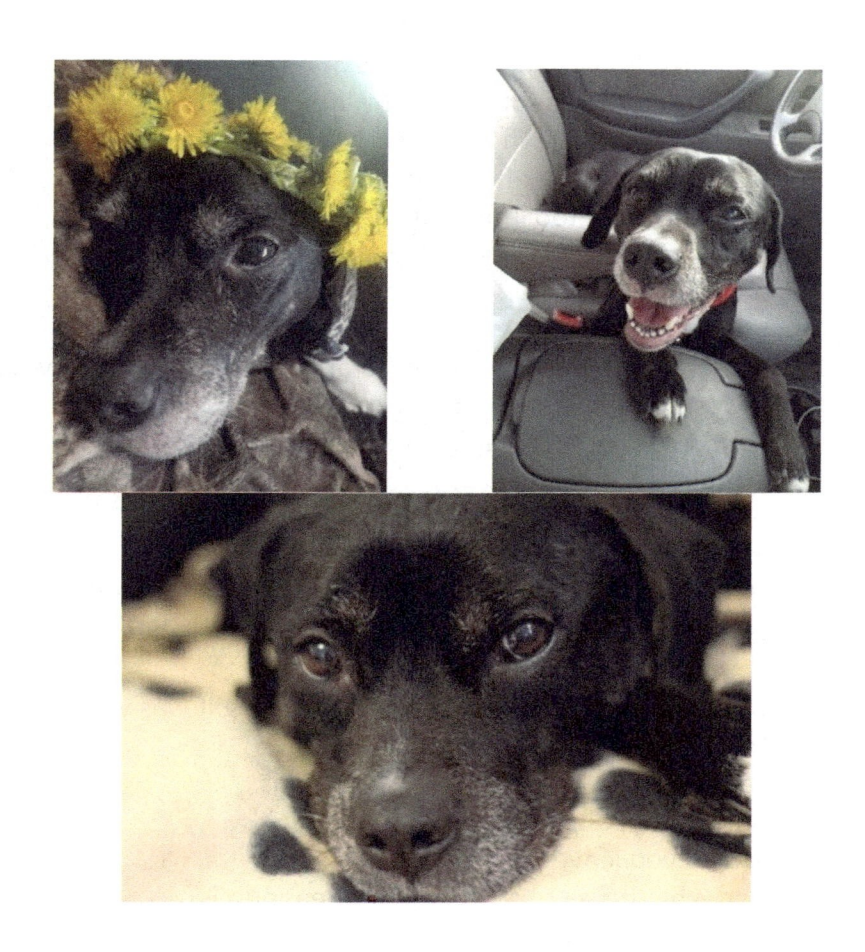

Dear Grandfather

Grandfather,
Is it okay to call you that?
What would you have had me call you?
Grandpa, Papa, Grandaddy, Pop...?
I've wondered about you all my life –
What you're like, who you are, how you looked.
I finally found you after years of searching,
But sadly, was too late. You passed away in 2018.
Funny story actually; growing up I already thought you were dead,
So did Daddy.
He even attended a man's funeral that he thought was you.
It wasn't until Grandpa S passed away that we
Found out you were actually alive and well,
Residing in New Mexico,
According to his obituary.
Imagine our surprise.
Naturally, I had so many questions and I tried to find you.
Like I said, by the time I finally did, it was only because I found
Your obituary with a picture.
Dad looks just like you, there's no denying it was you, haha...
I was only a baby when you left.
So now I'm left with so many questions...
Like, first of all, why?
Why'd you leave?
And why the secrecy of your whereabouts?
Weren't you curious?
Why'd you never try to contact Daddy? Make amends?
Try to reach out to me?
Funny, as far as I know you only knew about 6 of your grandchildren;
Myself and my 5 older cousins.
Well, there's 11 of us in total, and you even have quite a few great grandbabies.
I'm Daddy's oldest.

I've heard stories about you, but sadly, most of them weren't good...
But your obituary makes you sound like a very kind, good man that was active in his community.
So, I'm confused.
I'd like to have met you and made my own conclusions,
But all I have are stories.
And questions. So many questions.
Do you have a second family?
Do I have aunts or uncles that I don't know about?
I'd love to hear your stories.
What's our family history?
And medical issues I should worry about for Daddy? For myself?
What were your parents like?
What was Daddy like as a boy?
How'd you and Grandma meet?
I've heard you loved birds and had a ton of exotic ones in the house you built!
I too, love birds! I must have gotten that from you, I suppose?
Did you ever think about us?
Why'd you never come back?
Why New Mexico? What's there? What's it like?
I've always felt like a part of me is incomplete, missing, since I don't know much about our family,
Or you...
I wish I could have just one conversation with you
Get some answers, clarity, and closure.
Maybe one day I'll take a trip to Alamogordo,
See what's there, what it's like, what drew you to it.
Maybe I'll get to meet a few who knew you
And hear their stories.
Maybe one day we'll meet in another life
And I'll get to ask you my questions
But until then, farewell.
Sincerely,
The granddaughter you never knew

PuRe ChAoS

Dark.
Everything is so dark – and loud – chaotic.
I cannot see.
Fear.
Fear sets in and I'm afraid.
I'm afraid to close my eyes for
I know what waits for me on the other side.
The whirlwind of invasive thoughts and emotions that,
No matter what I do, I cannot keep them away!
It's like being forced to attend a party and it being demanded that you stay
So you stay even though you want to leave
But there's no escape!
Anxiety kicks in and there's no keeping it at bay!
Who invited you, anyway?
Stay.
Anxiety – depression's little brother that I felt obligated to bring to the party
But the party is my mind and try as I may
There's no way to escape
I'm afraid!
I'm afraid to speak up because when I do
I get labeled as crazy
And that's not okay!
But, I'm not okay!
And it's okay for me to not be okay!
But for fuck's sake
When *WILL* I be okay?!
I just want to feel happy
So I smile.
But I'm afraid.
I'm afraid of the fact that no one sees
When that smile fades
And everything that it hides
Simple.
Such a simple illusion, a wonderful façade
To fool the world with
And hide all the pain
A smile!
I'm afraid.

Thoughts of ending my life flood my brain
Death by suicide.
Death!
You'd think I'd be afraid of death, but no —
Death is easy, death is peace
There is no pain in death
Death does not make me afraid
What makes me afraid is living!
Living is hard!
This life that I'm told is mine
Yet, I have no control
Over anything, not even my own mind!
I'm at war.
A raging, constant battle that
I'm not even sure I can conquer
There's no way out without dying, anyway!
None of us make it out alive, so
Really, there's no real win
Just constant pain, suffering, and obstacles
To try to overcome & bear just long enough
To ultimately die!
So, in all actuality, death is the reward!
Death is the reward for all the pain we endured
And scars we earned during life, the chaotic mess
We finally get peace at death.
Death is peace, so no.
I am not afraid of death.
I am afraid of the incomparable pure chaos of life!
No! I am not afraid of death.
I'm afraid of living!

A letter to ALL who struggle...

First and foremost, YOU MATTER. YOU have PURPOSE. YOU are a BEAUTIFUL person! YOU belong HERE. YOU are LOVED. YOU are WORTHY! YOU are NEVER ALONE!

For those who have struggled, know someone who has struggled, or are currently struggling, this is for you. I have been in your shoes, and I will walk with you. I know it's hard; but do NOT give up, you have SO much to live for. I promise!

To anyone who has ever dealt with something heavy – this is for you! Let me take that weight off your shoulders and be your voice. You're never in this alone.

If you are looking to seek help, please reach out to any of the following:

1-800-273-TALK (8255... Veterans press 1)
Text "TALK" to 741741
Call or Text 988
You can also go online to www.988lifeline.org for an online chat option

For more information and resources, you can also visit the American Foundation for Suicide Prevention website at www.afsp.org

JUST BREATHE! Everything will be okay! You're so strong. You're so wonderful! You're not alone! Together, we'll make it through!

The following is my story and all that I've been through. There is talks of depression, suicide, abuse, rape, CPTSD, amongst others. Please read with caution if any of these triggers you. Please note, I first wrote this poem, I believe about 3 years ago, and have since revised it some. Not all that it contains applies to my current status. I've come very far in my healing journey, but I've left it as this is raw, this is real, and it's me. This is my story. I was nervous to release this, but I hope that it will shed some light on mental health and help those struggling see that they're not alone, put words to what they're feeling and going through, and overall help. That is always my goal. Thank you!

Hi! My Name Is...

Hello, I'm Aminika.
I have high-functioning anxiety.
It causes me to be a perfectionist and make sure every detail, big or small, is perfect.
It causes me to over-think everything and plan out my every move,
Often leading me to think the worst-case scenarios.
I apologize for everything, even when I am not wrong.
I worry too much, and I don't want to upset anyone.
I aim to always please and do my best to avoid conflict.
I fear arguments and am intimidated by raised voices.
I do not like loud noises or when too many people talk at once.
Bass hurts my head and throws off my sensory; too much noise throws me into a defensive state.
I have a noise sensory overload; it makes it hard to process.
I tend to not stand up for myself and bow down to others,
Often not doing what is best for me
And taking too much onto my plate.
I can't say "no", even when I want to or should.
I'm easily led to believe that I am worthless, and I always feel like others are judging me.
I aim to impress but always feel as though I fall short and fail; like I'm not enough.
I worry about what you, and everyone else, thinks about me.
I arrive early to my appointments in fear of being late and missing out, something going wrong, or simply the fear of being scolded.
I am listening to you, but I avoid making eye contact. It makes me nervous and uncomfortable.
This does not mean that I am lying or not paying attention.

It also does not mean that I lack knowledge in my statements.

It's just a part of my illness, and I need you to understand that it is not personal; I do not mean to "disrespect" you. I am trying to do well, but it makes me hot, red, and unable to clearly process my thoughts.

I am very intelligent and highly knowledgeable in a number of areas, but I fear public speaking. When I speak to a group, I tend to freeze up and my thoughts jumble as my mind races. What I want to convey to you may come out as a tornado of words, I may stutter and pause for long periods of time, or I may just stop talking.

Or - I may get super excited and talk way too much, way too fast, to the point you may feel you're at an auction! This does not mean that I am uneducated. I simply am anxious, frightened, and having a hard time processing my thoughts in a way that is easily communicated; but, if you give me a pen and paper, I will prove to you just how bright I truly am.

Please, don't think that I am "stupid" or "not paying attention" just because I freeze up when I do go to speak. I have so much to share with the world, and so much to offer, if you'll just work with me and give me a chance.

Yes, my desk and room are covered with sticky notes and dry-erase boards full of lists, ideas, and bits and pieces of random poetry that pops into my head. I also have multiple planners and organizers that you'll see me constantly using and writing in - color coordinated, of course! I try to organize my thoughts & things that I need to do - writing it out helps me.

I'm sorry if I ask you to repeat yourself a lot. It's not because I am not paying attention or because I believe what you're saying is unimportant. I just need to process what you said, again.

I have to try to always keep my mind busy, otherwise I fall into a trap and become prisoner of my own mind.

Please, don't find me weird for always twirling my hair around my fingers; it's just my way of calming myself down – often, I don't even realize I'm doing it.

I also carry and wear my crystals for my own benefits; I don't mean to offend you.

I tend to bite my lip, fidget with my ring, or play with a palm stone in my hand when I am nervous or stressed. Please don't take this as a sign of disrespect or me not listening to you if you're talking to me, that is not the case, and you have my undivided attention. It's just my way to soothe myself.

I'm sorry if I keep you awake at night; I have extreme difficulty falling and staying asleep. I don't mean to always be so tired and out of it, but the restless nights drain my energy and increase my forgetfulness. Please, bear with me when I need a few extra reminders.

I worry so much about the future and I need constant reassurance. I apologize if it annoys you that I may ask a lot of questions or always asking if everything is still okay with our friendship/relationship/whatever.

I'm sorry if I always ask if you still want me in your life, or if I come off too strong, or even insecure. Understand, so many have abandoned me when I *thought* everything was going great. So many have used me, drained me, and left me out to dry. I am afraid, but I am trying.

I replay conversations and scenarios in my head over and over, even from years ago. I'm sorry if I randomly bring things up or can't let something go – you must understand, my mind will literally not let me. Certain songs, places, names, sounds, and smells may trigger memories and cause this to heighten. It's not something I can control, and I apologize.

Keep in mind that your words hurt me more than you think.

Please choose your words, and actions, carefully. I latch on to every word and nothing goes unnoticed.

Please, do not send me a message and just say "we need to talk" or "there's a problem/accident" or anything among those lines. I need you to either tell me everything right then and there or wait until you see me. If not, it will eat away at me to uncontrollable limits, and I will go insane. Please understand, if I am open with you, I trust you a great deal. Please do not hurt me or use my confiding in you against me.

And please, my sickness is not a weapon to use against me. I'm sorry if I get jealous or ask if I'm still pretty – I'm just worried, my body is always changing, your thoughts and tastes are always changing. I just want to make sure we're on the same page.

I apologize if I always say I wish I looked a different way or put myself down; or if I call myself names, wish I was more successful or smarter. I compare myself to others often and rarely feel that I am beautiful in my own skin and mind.

I fear large gatherings and will often decline invites, especially to large parties. It's nothing at all against you, I just cannot handle it. I do not like big crowds, nor do I like the "party scene". I do, however, love music and concerts – but even those, I fear to go and often talk myself out of going – even for my favorite artists. So, I may need a little encouragement and reassurance, but I do <u>want</u> to go!

I procrastinate on everything because of stress and worries. The more I worry, the more I put off, the more overwhelmed I get, the more stressed I get, the more mentally crippled I become... it's a vicious cycle that seemingly has no end. Please, don't mistake this as a sign that I don't know what I'm doing, I do! I just get easily overwhelmed and I worry!

Hi! I'm Aminika. Yes, we've already met!
I suffer from depression.
I isolate myself because I don't know what else to do.
I don't mean to come across as rude or anti-social.

I don't mean to cut you off or push you away,
I just can't bear to let you see me like this... to hurt you or disappoint you!
Yes, I'm often "hiding" in my phone.
I'm not talking to anyone, it's just my escape... my safe place.
Typically, I'm playing a game, or browsing crystals and pagan stuff on Instagram; or
just browsing random shopping sites like Amazon, or my fave, Etsy!
I don't even purchase anything usually; I just make lots of wish lists because I need to distract my mind and keep the bad thoughts away.
Often even, I'm just jotting ideas and poems into my "notes".
Like I said, it's just my safe place.
Please, don't think I'm ignoring you - I'm actually paying very close attention.
I listen and observe well.
I do smile, and dance around, a lot, and I do laugh and tell jokes!
This is my way of coping and keeping myself safe; because I don't want you to see the dark & ugly reality that is me.
I laugh so that you don't ask.
I laugh so that I don't cry.
"You modeled - You were Miss. New York - You rode horses - You're beautiful ----- how are you depressed?"
Yes, it's true. I did do all those things, and I may be "beautiful".
But it doesn't change what I feel inside.
I must admit, the one photo that I'm most recognized for and am smiling in... I was also the most broken.
Modeling is silent acting... and I've become an expert at hiding my true emotions and faking a pretty smile/face and holding my head high.

If anything – the years of pageantry and modeling trained me how to make people see what I want them to see; and hide the painful truth.
So yes, I did those things.
It didn't change anything.
I just put on my mask, painted my smile, and plowed right through.
Nobody knew.
Master of disguise.
Yes, I cancel plans last minute!
My depression kicks in and I chicken out. It causes me to believe that you don't *really* want to see me, or even *talk* to me – that you just feel obligated to.
Ah, an anxious mind... sigh.
Yes, I sleep a lot. Actually... funny story, I really don't *sleep* much at all. I lay in bed and stare at the walls for hours on end while my restless mind races a billion miles a minute – I can't even keep up with my thoughts.
Often, I silently cry myself to sleep.
Sleep, ah, sleep... yeah, that didn't last long
Because next thing I know he's in my room and I'm a kid again –
My throat burns, my body hurts, my face is soaked and wet.
I awaken, screaming and crying, body shaking!
"Leave me alone!" It's him. I'm reliving the worst of my life all over again.
I kick and punch and scream, tossing my body, creating a tsunami in my bed sheets.
"Get the fuck off me! MOM!!!!"
I scream as loud as my meek, tired, trembling voice will allow. Can *anyone* hear me?
"Wait, babe? Oh! Babe!! Hold me... hold me, please?"
"No, get off me!! Get off me! I hate you! Stop! You're ripping my favorite night gown! Stop!! Leave me alone!" I

try to kick as hard as I can, tossing and turning my body as best as I can.

"Oh, shit, wait, babe? Babe, I'm so sorry! Hold me, please? Make it stop! Please, just hold me... don't let me go..."

I can't breathe. I need water.

Ah... okay. It's been an hour. I'm calmer now, but I'm afraid and wide awake. Why go back to sleep when I know what's waiting to unfold in my subconscious mind every time I close my eyes?

Oh. The moon. She's beautiful tonight.

She'll keep me company again.

I don't want him to come back, so, I toss and turn like the sea the rest of the night - my mind wondering and racing, yet it goes so silent.

What's that?

Uhg.

Sunlight.

It's morning again. I'm so tired.

It's exhausting.

I have such a hard time even getting out of bed. Often, simple things like just taking a shower or eating a meal takes all I've got and I'm ready for a nap after... and it's only 8AM.

Now wait... what's that now?

You want me to go to work?

Five days a week!?

EIGHT HOUR DAYS?!

Oh... I must or I won't be able to survive?!

But... I already can't survive...

What's that?

It's all in my head?

I'm being a whinny little bitch?

Mental health doesn't matter and isn't an excuse?

Oh.... okay...

I push through my day... after day... after day...

Wait, what day is it?

Depression is mentally and physically exhausting.
Often, it leaves me feeling like I just did a triathlon, or got my ass handed to me in the ring of a MMA match.
Yeah, exhausting. I know.
I'm always drained.
I never feel "good".
Y'all just don't understand how much depression affects me physically. My head hurts, my back & shoulders ache, my chest is tight...
I'm tired and can never catch a break!
I can go from being "okay", to being an absolute wreck in the blink of an eye... sometimes, I won't even know why.
I'll lose interest easily, even in things I love.
Often, there is no trigger - I cannot control it. Usually, it's without warning.
I'm sorry, and I'm trying.
I don't mean to always look sad or upset, or to be a "buzzkill".
I want to have fun...
Laugh & live, just like you.
It's just harder for me.
I need constant reminders that I am not alone; that I am not a bother.
I fear reaching out, and so, if I do, please understand that it took a lot - usually hours or even days of me planning and fighting with myself to actually do so.
And I trust you.
Trust... that's hard for me.
Please know that when I do reach out, I'm in the most uncomfortable and vulnerable state of being.
I'm stubborn, I can't stand to admit that I need help, and I don't like to feel like a burden.
So please, sit down and talk with me. I just need a little of your time, love, patience, and reassurance that everything will be okay... that *I* will be okay...

That I've made it through worse storms, and, as my favorite movie character would say, that "it can't rain all the time". Sometimes, I forget to eat. Okay often. Very often I forget to eat. I'm just not hungry and often don't want anything. Then, sometimes I can feel my stomach aching - but I don't have it in me to even get up & get food for myself. Then, there's times where all I want to do is eat away my feelings & I usually overeat - resulting in my beating myself up for gaining weight & feeling like shit for over-eating.
I have a poor relationship with food.
A lot of the time I'm indecisive, I don't know what I want. I've got likes and interests, but often my depression, alongside it's sidekick: my anxiety, blocks it and I just lose interest and don't want anything. Please understand, it's not personal, I'm just really bad at keeping in touch with people. I try, but then my anxiety gets the best of me, and I get to thinking that I'm annoying or am a burden. I think about my friends & family often, and I do mean to reach out - it just usually quickly becomes overwhelming. Just know that I care, I do love you, and I'm always here - silently watching from a far - rooting for you.
My home is usually an organized mess; like I know where things are, but it's still a mess. My anxiety makes the tasks of cleaning & organizing feel very overwhelming, impossible, and honestly, even scary. I never know where to start - living room? Bathroom? My room? Kitchen? Laundry? Dishes? Where!? - my head becomes clouded and it becomes impossible to focus on one task at a time - nothing really seems to get done and I end up getting frustrated - then, my depression sets in and I ultimately end up giving up "until tomorrow" - ah, yes, the "until tomorrow" ... a ruthless concatenation of events without an end.
There are times that I'll go days without speaking to anyone. I'm just so lost within myself and trapped inside.

You may think I'm ignoring you, but I promise I'm not. I don't mean to push you away; actually, this is one of the times I need you the most.
"You have pets". Yes, I do have pets. They are my life support. They make it **easier**, but they do not make it all **disappear**.
Often, I will go for walks alone (Ok, ok. With my dog!). It's my way to calm my thoughts and ground myself. Often if I'm upset, I will just walk away, typically without saying a word. Please don't take it personally, it's just how I cope. If you're worried about me, please don't hesitate to follow me, but sometimes I just need to walk and not talk. Your presence and concern are both appreciated. Thank you.

Hey, I'm Aminika. Yes, we've met before.
I suffer from CPTSD, but you probably already guessed that.
As you can see, my illnesses bleed into each other. Great, right? Sigh.
Something you need to understand firstly is that PTSD is not just something that soldiers face, and CPTSD and PTSD are slightly different.
PTSD is related to a single event and goes away with time, whereas CPTSD is related to a series of events, or one prolonged event.
I have a hard time maintaining healthy and strong connections with my friends & loved ones. This is of course in no way meant to be taken personally.
I'm in a constant state of hyperarousal - jumpy & easily startled, usually always on edge and high alert.
I'm always looking around & aware of all my exits and who/what is around me and where things are. I have a constant fear that someone is going to hurt me, because sadly in the past, that was true. I now proceed through life with caution. I've witnessed so much and have been through too much, so please be gentle when making physical

contact with me; and try to let me know you're near before touching me.

I have extremely vivid flashbacks - but you probably already noted that... both when I'm asleep, and sometimes when I'm awake, it's there. Sometimes I may seem like I'm dazed, and I may jump when coming back to reality. I apologize if I zone out,

I also wake up, screaming and crying, I apologize if I wake you, I don't mean to! Please understand, to you it may be just a dream, to me, in that moment, it's real, and it's happening all over again. You must understand, I LIVED it - it's not just a random dream or flashback. And each and every time they happen, it's like I'm re-living it all, again, and again, and again...

Often, I feel dizzy and not wish to move, and or feel nauseous. There are times I may actually vomit if I get too worked up and reminded too much of my traumas, especially after a dream episode.

Certain songs and shows are too much for me to handle, and I may ask you to change it - or I may just walk away. If I'm in a group with multiple people, I may do what I can to disconnect myself for the duration of whatever it is we're doing and find something to distract myself and disassociate from the trigger. Typically, it will be putting on my headphones and listening to my favorite music or podcast (Psst, shout out to Good for You, Camp Cryptid, & Dark History! Just a few of my faves!). I'm not trying to be rude; I just want to avoid triggers and invasive thoughts! There are many places and situations that I will avoid because they remind me and bring me back to traumatic events I've had to live through. Please understand that if there is a certain place that you'd wish for me to go with you or something you'd like us to do together that I say no to due to this, please don't call be a "coward" or a "wuss" or any other name you think of, or tell me that I need to "get over it" or "face my fears", etc.... I am not ready, and I will work at my own pace to overcome my fears. I don't want to cause myself more trauma or re-open wounds that I'm not ready to face.

And **please** understand; I'm **not** afraid of the *dark* - what I'm afraid of is not being able to see **in** the dark, due to past experiences. I need to have a little light & be able to clearly see at all times - so yes, I sleep with a small night light. I need to feel safe.

I am startled by loud, unexpected noises and raised voices - please just give me a moment to process what's happening & gather my thoughts and emotions. I also do not like people in my face or coming at me quickly. I do not like being touched without permission - it alarms me and takes me a second to figure out how to react; so please, bear with me.

I have extreme trust issues - I beg you not to take it to heart; it's just that too many that I've loved and cared about, who also claimed to love me, have burned me, so I've set up a wall for my own protection.

It takes a lot to gain my trust, and it takes consistent work to keep it; especially if you've broken it before.

Yes, at times I may have a negative view of myself due to my trauma and there are many things that I may believe I'm unworthy of, or that I'm not beautiful. This self-sabotaging mind set is something I'm consistently battling with and actively working on correcting - I'm trying to get better.

I just need time, and, at times, a friendly hand to hand me the bricks and help me build my castle. I need a strong support team of positive, like-minded, motivated people - so please, if you're just going to try to tear me down, I need you to stay away from me.

Yes, I battle with suicidal thoughts, no, this does not make me selfish, weak, or a bad person!

No, I will not shut up! These are the conversations that need to be had! Do not try to silence me!

Yes, when I believe someone or something may hit me, I cringe. Even if it's in a playful manor.

Yes, I may not answer my phone for periods of times, or I may barricade myself in my home & not come out for a few days at a time. Sure, I may bury myself in a book or absorb my time with writing what may feel like a novel. All of this may seem abnormal to you, but for me, this is self-care. These are some of my coping mechanisms.

And, while we're on the subject, yes you will more often than not find me with headphones on. Music is my most powerful coping tool & it helps me the most. This does not mean that I'm ignoring you or that I cannot hear you — I can and I'm not trying to be rude — I just really need my music.

Big rooms scare me. Classrooms get my nerves through the roof which yes, made high school and college difficult at times. Yes, I try to be invisible. City buses give me anxiety attacks, walking new streets makes me nervous. Taking a new route scares me. New environments and big moves are very hard for me. Yet, you probably wouldn't guess it, but I actually like change & I embrace it, even though it's difficult for me! I like to be challenged.

Everyday life is hard for me, sure. Things that seem so nonchalant are things that I struggle with & fear. Please just, let me move at my own pace & work *with* me, not *against* me.

Please, don't tell me to "just relax" or "get over it" ... trust me, if it were that easy, I'd have done it a long time ago! I do not like that I am this way, but it's something I must work at and deal with and learn to do my best in living with. This is my realty.

Hi, I'm Aminika.
And I am NOT my illness. Yes, these things are true, and I must deal with them, but these things do not define me! Hi. I'm Aminika. Allow me to re-introduce myself.

Hi. I'm Aminika. I am a poet and an artist.
Hi. I'm Aminika. I have a full-time job and thrive there.
Hi. I'm Aminika. I'm a photographer
Hi. I'm Aminika. I make candles, perfumes, beard products, and hair/body oils.
Hi. I'm Aminika. I am a trade-school graduate.
Hi. I'm Aminika. I am an empath; I can feel everything.
Hi. I'm Aminika. I'm a proud fur (and scale!) mommy!
Hi. I'm Aminika. I am a loving stepmother to 3 beautiful children!
Hi. I'm Aminika. I am a girlfriend. A best friend. A sister. A daughter.
Hi. I'm Aminika. I love to hike, to read, to cook, to explore, to learn, to see the world!
Hi. I'm Aminika. I have a major soft spot for animals.
Hi. I'm Aminika. I'm an axe-throwing badass!
Hi. I'm Aminika. I love to ride horses.
Hi. I'm Aminika. I am a devout pagan.
Hi. I'm Aminika. I wear my weaknesses as armor so they cannot be used against me.
Hi. I'm Aminika. I am a survivor.
Hi. I'm Aminika. And I am so much more.

About the Author

Aminika Lee grew up in the small town of Watervliet, New York. She was introduced to poetry at a young age and immediately fell in love with it. In the fifth grade, there was a poetry contest which her teacher had the class submit their poetry to. Aminika's poem, *I See You Everywhere*, (which is included in this book just as a "what started it all" kind of deal) was one of the selected poems to be published into a poetry collection book. From there on, there was no stopping her. Aminika found comfort in poetry. Her junior and senior year in high school is where she really dove in headfirst with the encouragement of her junior and senior year English teachers, Ms. Cahill and Mr. Snyder. Still to this day, she can often be found scribbling down on sticky notes bits and pieces, or even full out poems, that pop in her head throughout her day — as with the case with her 2022 poem *The Voyage*!

Beyond poetry, growing up Aminika was an active child/teen. She had a rough at home life, so she enjoyed being involved in sports and after school clubs and activities. She played softball, basketball, tennis, and did cheerleading. She also participated in many of her school's after school clubs such as S.A.D.D., Reality Check (A youth-lead, adult supported movement against Big Tobacco), Art Club, the school newspaper, and was a class representative and part of her student council.

She rode horses, on and off as she could, which is her truest love. Aminika has a deep love for music; being heavily influenced by her favorite band Evanescence and their front woman Amy Lee, as well as Three Days Grace. She also is a huge fan of Reba, Garth Brooks, Chris Young, Shania Twain, Kane Brown, Peyton Parrish, SKÁLD, Wardruna, Brantley Gilbert, Eminem, Chester Bennington/Linkin Park, Poison, Ozzy Osbourne, Jesse McCartney, Tom MacDonald, Nova Rockafeller, and Dax, — all from whom she has been inspired but especially when she listens to Tom, Nova, (shout out to this incredible independent power couple!) and Eminem and sees the poetic patterns, word play, lines that have double, triple, and quadruple meanings that blow her mind, and the overall deep craft that goes into the words to the music she listens to. She has always obsessed over the lyrics to her favorite songs and heavily got into writing her own lyrics, which deepened her passion for poetry. Adding to her love of music, she has also spent some time dabbling in guitar, drums, violin, and piano. Her dream is to learn piano well enough to write her own music. She is also a huge fan of live music and is a big concert enthusiast, nothing ignites a spark in her soul like a fantastic show and powerful music! She has even met some of her favorites, including Dustin Lynch on more than one occasion and Kane Brown! She has also seen her favorite band, Evanescence, live, but has not met her biggest idol, Amy Lee (*yet!!!*).

Aminika also has a deep love and appreciation for stand-up comedy; along with loving the atmosphere and enjoying a good laugh – she admires the craft and structure of a good story line for bits and the creativity. She is a big Whitney Cummings fan, as well as Gabriel "Fluffy" Iglesias, Matt Rife, Kevin Hart, Michael Jr., and she likes to follow Dry Bar Comedy on YouTube.

Aminika has also always had a passion and love for photography that went right along with her poetry, for just about as long, if not longer. She joined her school's photography club, and her senior year she went on to complete multiple photography internships. From there, she proceeded to launch Bella Luna Photography in 2011 and continued photography classes. In 2015, she graduated from The New School Center for Media, completing their program in Television and Video Production (which also heavily focused on still photography) as well as their Advanced Animation and Graphic Design Program.

Aminika has also modeled for 10+ years and done pageantry; even going as far as winning the Miss. New York title for more than one pageant system throughout her years!

Aminika has a deep love for the arts; she is responsible for all the art and photographs within this book! Aminika has been drawing, painting, carving, you name it, since 9th grade when she was first introduced to her middle/high school art teacher Mrs. Lavick, who she'd go on to take more art classes with. She also likes to dabble in makeup artistry – especially anything unique, grungy and wild! She is a huge Halloween buff and loves the opportunity to show off her fun makeup looks, *without* getting weird looks from others!

Today, Aminika has a full-time job but keeps herself very busy with creative outlets, poetry and photography included, hikes with her family and her dog, and enjoys attending car shows! She also very much enjoys hand-making candles, bath salts, beard balms, hair & skin oils, and perfumes!

Want to check out more of Aminika's different works? She posts her photography on Instagram and Facebook as well as her candles and other creations! Find her below:

Bella Luna Photography:

@bellalunaphotographyy

www.facebook.com/bellalunaphotographyy

Creations by Ami Lee:

@creationsbyamilee

www.facebook.com/creationsbyamilee

Made in the USA
Columbia, SC
05 April 2025